Melodies of Life Of a Blue Rose

Echo's from a Blue Rose

Melodies of Life Of a Blue Rose

Echo's from a Blue Rose

Dipankur Bodwal

ISBN : 978-93-340-3218-5

Book Cover by- Dipankur Bodwal

Any references to historical events, real people, or real places are used fictitiously. Names, characters, and places are products of the author's imagination.

First printing edition 2024.

Dipankur Bodwal

dipankurbodwal@gmail.com

dipankurbodwal@yahoo.com

A Tribute

In the embrace of the celestial sky, under the whispering leaves of ancient trees, amidst the symphony of birdsong and the gentle caress of the wind, I dedicate this humble offering to the boundless wonders of nature and the intricate fabric of human emotions.

To the verdant forests that cradle secrets untold, and the majestic mountains that stand as silent sentinels of time, I offer my gratitude for inspiring the essence of life itself. Each petal of the blue rose, kissed by the morning dew, carries within it the essence of your grace and resilience.

To the ethereal dance of sunlight upon rippling waters, and the tranquil beauty of a moonlit night, I bow in reverence to your ever-changing canvas, painting the world with hues of serenity and passion.

In the labyrinth of the human heart, where love and longing intertwine, where joy and sorrow weave their intricate dance, I find solace and inspiration. It is in the depths of our emotions that the true essence of our existence is revealed, where every tear shed and every smile shared becomes a testament to our humanity.

This book, "Melodies of Life of a Blue Rose," is a journey into the depths of both nature's splendor and the human soul. It is a celebration of the delicate balance between fragility and strength, between vulnerability and resilience. May its pages serve as a tribute to the profound connection between the natural world and the infinite complexity of our hearts.

With profound reverence and boundless gratitude.

Dipankur Bodwal

In the heart of twilight's gentle sigh,
Where stars alight and dreams drift nigh,
There lies a tale, Yet to be told,
Of secrets whispered, of mysteries untold.

In whispers soft, the wind conveys,
The tales of night, in moonlight's haze,
Where shadows dance and echoes roam,
In the silent realm of the twilight's dome.

Each breath of air, a whispered song,
Echoing the truths that have long been gone,
In the fabric of dusk's embrace,
Lies the essence of time and space.

So let us wander, in this moonlit night,
Where dreams take flight and hearts sees soul in sight.

For in the silence of the fading light,
Lies the mysteries of the coming night.

In the quiet cradle of dawn's gentle light,
A blue rose stirs, yet to unfurl his might.
With petals closed tight, he waits to bloom,
Heeding the wind's whispers, in nature's room.

In the hushed anticipation of his nascent form,
The blue rose listens, to the wind's warm.
Promising tales of skies vast and wide,
Where dreams take flight, on freedom's tide.

As a child, the blue rose leans,
On tales whispered by wind and streams.
It seems, though these stories may not be true,
For a child, they weave dreams anew.

In sunshine's embrace, hope blooms bright,
Unaware of worries, in his innocent flight.
Listening to the wind's fairytales with glee,
The blue rose dances in dreams, carefree.

Guided by whispers of the gentle breeze,
he lingers, in stillness, beneath the trees.

As time wanders on, the blue rose unfurls,
Longing to bloom, The nature shows his spirit a
new room.

He queries the soil, "When shall I ascend,
To greet the heavens, as my journey begins?"

With new hopes kindled, and beginnings anew,
In the innocence of youth, like a child, his inquires
true.

The blue rose ponders the mysteries untold,
A treasure of nature, waiting to unfold.

But the soil whispers, a gentle reply,
"Patience, dear rose, beneath the sky.
Though now you're young, your time will come,
To spread your wings, beneath the sun."

The blue rose waits, with hope and grace,
Trusting the soil, in its embrace.
For though he longs to fly, to reach the sky,
He knows in time, he too will fly.

With the dawn's gentle kiss, blue petals unfurl,
The long-awaited moment, the rose's own swirl.

In the embrace of sunlight, he blooms anew,
As dreams take flight, in the morning dew.

The blue rose, tuned to bird songs' sweet call,
Ponders: are they friends or foes, one and all?
Yearning to befriend them, every chirp and trill,
He beckons the wind, to seek them out, with skill.

His old companion, the wind, softly calls,
Inviting the rose to befriend the rain that falls.
For in his heart, the rain's touch remains,
A silent song, amid nature's refrains.

Though never spoken, his longing is clear,
For the rain's gentle touch, to linger near.
Hoping that in silence, the rain may stay,
And in her presence, the blue rose may sway.

As a child, the blue rose watches, The world's worries, Unaware of the truth, in his innocent flurries.

For worries are but tales, woven with fear,
Memories of past, drawing near.

In his joyous bloom, he knows no fears,
No worries to cloud his tender years.
For in the forest embrace, he finds delight,
Basking in the warmth of morning light.

With each petal unfurled, in hues so bold,
The blue rose's innocence, a story to be told.
In this innocence, he discovers his grace,
Unburdened by worries, in this sacred space.

The blue rose's innocence, a sight to behold.
In his innocence, he finds life unfold,
The silent place nature hold.
Amidst the forest embrace, he dances with glee,
A symbol of purity, for all to see.

With petals reaching toward the vast expanse,
The blue rose ponders in a silent essence.
Curious of the sky, where dreams may roam,
In his quest for answers, he finds a home.

Observing the ever-changing shades above,
The blue rose feels the boundless love.
In the canvas of the heavens, he finds allure,
knowing this, blue rose feels evermore secure.

For in the vast open skies,
The blue rose sees where true beauty lies.
No need for dreams with open eyes,
The sky's colors deep,
Everlasting hues in which secrets sleep.

With clouds as brushes, painting shades divine,
Life's brilliance gleams in the sun's design.

A blue rose sings, mysteries of life our soul brings,
In the dance of existence, we find our role,
Senses awaken, each a lively scroll.
Life's purpose revealed in every touch,
A symphony of sensations, are as such.

The soul of soil, in his silent might,
Nurtures the seeds, igniting our flight.
The breeze of wind, a gentle embrace,
Guides us onward, with effortless grace.

The sun, a beacon, our heart's steady drum,
Pulsing with rhythm, where all things become.
Water, a vessel, holding souls untold,
Binding us together, a story unfold.

In the web of being, our minds explore,
Shaping the world, as never before.
With each breath we take, nature's truth revealed,
in the curtains of life, our fate sealed.

In the forest of dreams, a blue rose sways,
Whispered secrets in the breeze's gentle haze.
Beneath the cold sun's distant gaze,
Our souls try to find solace in its mysteries and maze.

In this icy realm, where shadows loom,
Our eyes perceive the hue, breaking through the gloom.
With emotions unnamed, yet deeply felt,
We paint our moments, where words may melt.

For there are feelings beyond the verbal art,
Sensations too profound, tearing worlds apart.
In the silence of hearts, they quietly brew,
A rose so blue, where our soul find shadows anew.

From the eyes of blue rose, In life's untold mystery, intent unfold souls so true, Each moment a canvas for the words we paint through.

Absurd they may seem, without clear meanings, words of selfless means.

Yet they echo despair and joy of beings.
In nature's symphony, they find their place,
Sounds of silence, each with its grace.

From whispers of wind to the songs of stream, Words merge with the world, in a shimmering gleam.

Through words, we attempt to explain,
The depths of our hearts, our sorrows and pain.

But in the noise of this world, They're but fleeting things, Mere echoes of souls in the dance that life brings.

A blue rose sees, life's canvas, rich with hues so vast, Yet trouble brews when desires are cast.

Seeking to alter shades it's our will that say,
Heavy heart remains, when the acts of shades don't come to play.

Maze of expectations in life's flow,
As colors refuse to blend and grow.
Frustration mounts when visions stray,
From the vivid dreams we long to portray.

But perhaps therein lies the beauty untold,
In embracing the hues that life unfolds.
For in the unexpected, true wonders reside,
An ocean of colors, where our souls subside.

So let us not lament when shades don't align,
But revel in the spectrum, divine and fine.
For life's true essence lies not in control,
But in the ever-changing colors of the soul.

As the blue rose's listens, a symphony of melodies, captivating and free. Amidst fluttering butterflies and buzzing insects, Nature's orchestra plays, a harmonious dialect.

Within his petals, a tale of solitude may dwell,
Yet in his silence, emotions weave their spell.
For amidst a broken heart, where raindrops fall,
And in the moonlight's song, where streams call.

Where words can be indecisive, lost in the fray,
Feelings unspoken, in silence they lay.
With tears unshed, and expressions concealed,
Invisible emotions, to others unrevealed.
His eyes, filled with hidden bliss, gaze above,
At the clouds that soar, in skies they love.

In the silent depths of the blue rose's hue,
Resides a truth untainted and true.

His quiet presence speaks to the soul mysteries untold, Beyond what words, in their stories, unfold.

In the realm of dreams, a blue rose sighs,
Beneath the moonlit sky, he softly lies.
In whispered reveries, he paints the scene,
Of nature's dance, both gentle and serene.

Through storms and rain, he learns to bend,
Resilient petals, with strength to mend.
Each droplet a kiss, each thunderous roar,
A testament to nature's ever-changing lore.

In the embrace of sun, he sits in delight,
Unfurling petals, radiant and bright.
Yet even in joy, a shadow may loom,
A reminder of life's transient bloom.

And in the cloak of night, he finds solace deep,
Amidst the silence, where secrets keep.
In solitude's embrace, he learns to grow,
Roots entwined with the ebb and flow.

For in the dreams of a blue rose, we see, Nature's intents, its canvas of time. A symphony of experiences, both dark and bright, guiding us through the journey of life’s flight.

In the dreams of the blue rose, lives curtain weaves, Threads of existence, where destiny cleaves.

Beyond storms and rain, beyond sun's warm embrace, Lie deeper truths, in the boundless space.

In the dance of life, birth's tender cry,
A symphony of beginnings, reaching for the sky.
Each moment a miracle, each breath a sacred song,
In the chorus of creation, we all belong.

But intertwined with life, death's gentle call,
A transition, where shadows fall.
In the stillness of night, where stars softly gleam,
A reminder of life's transient dream.

For in the dreams of the blue rose, we find,
The cycle of life, both gentle and kind.
From birth to death, in nature's maze,
A journey of souls, seeking eternal grace.

In the blue rose's gaze, the stream cascades,
A soothing melody, where serenity pervades.
Untold questions linger, in the depths untamed,
Yet the stream whispers secrets, unnamed.

With answers lost in the streams that flow,
Nature's wisdom speaks, in a language we know.
Astray we wander, in the wilderness vast,
Seeking truths elusive, as shadows cast.

But in the gentle babbles of the world, truths unfold, In the stream's quiet tears, a song that is old, where mysteries of life untold.

For in the untamed wilds, where dreams take flight,
Nature's song guides us, through the darkest night.

In the blue rose's eyes, the sky stretches wide,
A canvas of dreams, where hopes reside.

But grounded in soil, he longs to soar,
To touch the heavens, forevermore.

With no wings to carry, his dreams aloft, in stillness, Despite the soft whispers of autumn in life's forgetfulness.

Nearing his last breath blue rose call,
A final wish, before the petals fall.

Watching the birds, with envy and sigh,
Feelings that could fly, yet expressions become shy.

For in his heart, fears reside,
Of making dreams into falsehood's guide.

In the blue rose's quiet grace,
There lies a truth, in the fleeting space.
For dreams may falter, dreams may die,
But within each petal, they still lie.

For even as autumn's breath draws near,
The blue rose's dream remains clear.

In the heart's flight, he finds his home,
A testament to dreams that roam.

In the blue rose's view, seasons unfold,
Each with a story, both new and old.
With an open heart, he embraces the change,
Finding beauty in the vast and the strange.

From spring's gentle bloom
To winter's frosty gloom,
The blue rose witness,
With a quiet wistfulness.
In the dance of the seasons, he finds his part,
A silent observer, with a beating heart.

Amidst the nature's sound, the blue rose stands still, his roots deep in the ground.

Even silence has sound, In the heart of calmness, where words can't speak yet emotions profound.

For in the silence that follows, a wish comes true,
In the stillness, where dreams renew.
In the quiet of the night, under starlit skies,
The blue rose finds solace, where silence lies.

The blue rose listens to the calming music the wind brings, As a cold wave starts and the snow softly sings.

New songs emerge in the crisp winter air, And the blue rose is enchanted by the melodies rare.
Warmer than words in the freezing chill,
Emotions unsaid, yet they echo still.
They sing a song to melt the icy cold,
As the blue rose's heart, their beauty, unfold.

In the cold air, the heart finds warmth in the songs the blue rose hears,
A wondrous snow blankets the land, Painting winter's beauty clear.

Though colors may not dance within the snow's pure white, It spreads the shades of truth, an enchanting sight.

In moments of solitude, the true forms unfold,
Revealing the essence of life, in hues untold.
The blue rose sees in the snow's pristine hue,
The colors of truth, preserved in his soul, anew.

Watching the sunrise in the morning snow,
Brings colors anew, a vibrant show.
As the blue rose sees, he unfurls his soul,
To the melody of dawn, making it whole.

Leaving a song, no words can describe,
The sky so blue, like petals imbibe.
The rose dances with the wind, in graceful flight,
Singing songs for winter, in the morning light.

As the sun ascends, painting skies with gold,
The rose drinks in the beauty, uncontrolled.
For in this moment, he finds his place,
Amidst nature's symphony, a sacred space.

With each breath of crisp, winter air,
The blue rose feels alive, without a care.
For in the embrace of snow and light,
He discovers joy, pure and bright.

In the snow, a stranger wanders near,
With silent steps, words of wisdom appear.
From distant lands, a face unknown,
A deer emerges, the trees have shown.

In its soulful eyes, a moment held,
Silent steps of time, a story compelled.
Leaving each moment to become a past untold,
The blue rose watches, his petals unfold.

In the quiet moments of present, the future veiled,
Unseen paths in the snow, where mysteries hailed.
Trails of the past, left by the deer's grace,
Leave hope for the future, in this silent embrace.

Though the path ahead may not be clear,
The past's fading echoes, whispers near.
The blue rose observes, in silent awe,
As the deer's journey unfolds, without flaw.

In nature's boundless library, the blue rose roams,
Where each page holds the secrets of life's tones.
Amidst wind in the babble of stream,
He finds solace and belonging,
in nature's sacred dream.

With petals unfurled, he immerses in the forest's embrace, Where every creature, every leaf, tells a tale of grace.

In the symphony of life, he hears his own refrain,
A melody of interconnectedness, a chorus without chain.

Beneath the starry sky, he contemplates the cosmic dance, Where each twinkling light holds a story of chance.

In nature's grand narrative, he finds his own place,
A verse in the poem of life, a fragment of grace.
And so, the blue rose embraces his role in nature's book, A chapter of mysteries, that the soul took.
For within these pages lies the essence of his soul,
A timeless tale of beauty, in nature's sacred scroll.

As the blue rose's sways, the wildflower blooms,
A companion in solitude, amidst nature's perfumes.

With no words exchanged, their bond undefined,
Yet in the hues that stand apart, a connection entwined.

Fear may whisper of a broken heart's plight, But the blue rose finds solace in the wildflower's light.

Alone, yet not lonely, in the wonders of life,
Joy shines bright, amidst struggle and strife.

In stillness, he speaks all, to the love he holds dear,
A silent declaration, in the presence so near.

For in the language of hearts, words need not be spoken, In the curtains of nature, love remains unbroken.

In the forest embrace, the blue rose stands, amidst the blooms, where nature's hand, paints fragrant hues, both bold and fair,
Yet unaware of the scent, he has in the air.

In the whispering breeze, he catches a scent,
Of rain-kissed air, where dreams are lent.
But in his quiet grace, doubts arise,
As he questions his worth under sunlit skies.

Silent and still, he longs to know,
If his fragrance too, has a gentle glow.
Yet in the chorus of blooms, he feels small,
Lost amidst voices, he cannot call.

Yet hidden within his petals' embrace,
Lies a fragrance rare, a gift of grace.
For in the heart of the blue rose, we find a beauty unique, Of the purest souls that speak.

Amid uncertainty, his uniqueness shines bright,
In nature's realm, a treasure of exquisite light.
For in his scent, untold stories unfold,
A testament to beauty, rare and bold.

In the forest, the blue rose found love,
in the rain's tender touch, from skies above.
Whispering songs, in the gentle downpour,
A symphony of love, forevermore.

The wind, a friend, brings the rain's sweet embrace,
Guiding clouds in a delicate chase.
With every breeze, the blue rose waits,
For the dance of clouds, at the forest's gates.
Yearning to be with the rain, he waits in delight,
For the clouds to gather, in the moonlit night.

In their union, a love story to be told,
In the forest's heart, where dreams unfold.
The blue rose awaits the rain's gentle call,
With a song in her fragrance, his heart stall.
He whispers to the wind, his trusted friend,
Of love as true as the song he penned.

Yet the rain delays, her arrival unknown,
And the blue rose's patience is tested, alone.
Still, he holds onto hope, in the scent of his bloom,
As he awaits the rain's sweet touch, in nature's vast room.

When rain arrives, the blue rose rejoice,
For the love song of nature, his voice.
In the rhythm of raindrops, his heart finds ease,
And sorrow fades, lost in the gentle breeze.

With each tender note, the blue rose sways,
In the symphony of rain, he finds his place.
Though dreams may linger, silent and still,
In the embrace of rain, his soul fulfills.

For in the quiet of the shower's grace,
The blue rose finds solace, in nature's embrace.
Silent as the starry night,
Yet filled with love's delight,
In the rain's sweet melody, he finds respite.
The blue rose sings,
Unfurling his petals, the fragrance he brings.

His petals, the windows to his soul,
Reveal his love to the rain, as she begins to roll.
Though the rain's response may be delayed,
In this moment, the blue rose's love is displayed.
For he seeks not the duration of the shower,
But to share his love, in this fleeting hour.

In the hush of dawn, the blue rose sighs,
As the rain bids farewell with tearful eyes.
"Stay a little longer," the rose implores,
"Let us linger in the moment, on nature's shores."

But the rain must depart, moment call,
Leaving behind memories, like teardrops that fall.
The blue rose reaches out, to touch her soul,
Yet the rain withdraws, with a silent toll.

"Don't look at me like this," the rain pleads,
"For your gaze holds me captive, in love's needs."
But the rain knows the truth, in her heart's refrain,
That their time together is but a fleeting gain.

With gentle hands of droplets, she brushes away,
The words of longing on lips, that the blue rose may say.
"I cannot linger," the rain softly replies, "For our love is bound by the tears in our eyes."

Yet in the silence of their parting embrace,
The blue rose finds solace, in love's grace.

For though the rain may leave, her essence remains,
In the whispered memories, where love sustains.

And so they part, in the quiet of the morn,
The blue rose and the rain, forever reborn.
Their love transcends time, in nature's art,
As they dance together, in each other's heart.

The rain puts her hand on the blue rose, halting him to speak, As the winds of change whisper, in the rain's mystique.

Time heeds not the hearts that ache and yearn,
Yet the raindrops remain, a symbol of love's return.

Though the rose waits, watching the rain fade away,
The pain in his eyes, hidden by tears that stray.

For in the absence of rain, the sorrow deepens its hold, In the lonely souls, where love's story is told.

When the rain departs, the blue rose stands alone,
in the silent, windy night, his presence shone.
Awaiting the return of the rain's sweet sway,
in solitude, he lingers, night and day.

When love departs, leaving the heart in pain,
The blue rose stand still, longing for the rain.
He cannot reveal his sorrow to the world's eye,
but within raindrops, his tears may lie.

Concealed within shadows, in the rain's tender heart, the blue rose finds solace, as she departs.
For in the rain's embrace, he finds his release,
Hiding his tears, in nature's peace.
In the hush of silence, longing unfurls,
As raindrops turn to tears, for the blue rose's world.

Unfair it may seem, their departure so swift,
leaving behind a soul adrift.
Unable to make the rain stay, yet feeling rain's embrace, as she nurture the soul with heart's grace.
In the quiet of the night, mysteries unfold,
as the blue rose's story remains untold.

The blue rose longing to meet again, love's silent pain, in the scorching days of summer's reign.
As the rain brings her love to the blue rose's core,
A silent longing, forevermore.

The blue rose yearns to see the rain, to feel her grace, to be enveloped in rain's embrace.
Letting rain blend in the forest's hues, creating a painting, born of blue rose muse.

You, a candle with flames of love, guiding me through darkness, from above. Wherever you are,
There I'll be, bound by eternity, in unity.

Blue rose and rain, entwined in life's dance,
Their canvas adorned with joy and chance.
Each brushstroke a moment, each color a tale,
A bond of blue rose and rain, beyond the pale.

In the gallery of time, painting shall stand,
A reflection of love, hand in hand.
For blue rose and rain, forever entwined,
In the colors of life, their souls aligned.

In the lingering essence of rainbows, the blue rose gleams, Captured in vibrant hues, he wistfully dreams.

Each color holds a memory, each arc a sigh,
In the blue rose's forest, dreams ascend high.

Though the rain has departed, her fragrance remains still, in the rainbow's glow with a serene, soulful thrill.

In this tranquil emotion, devotion finds its hold,
As the blue rose's spirit, in rainbow, unfolds.
As the sun emerges, painting skies anew,
The blue rose basks in nature's renew.

With each petal kissed by the morning dew,
He knows that in nature's embrace, dreams come true.

To the animals in the forest, the blue rose speaks,
Of love's whispers, where solace seeks.
Silent and listen, the same letters they share,
In the quiet, love's presence, beyond compare.

Love is born of understanding, it's true,
Nourished by emotions, in shades of blue.
In its embrace, no room for conclusion,
Just the merging of souls, in sweet fusion.

Like solute and solvent in a solution's kiss,
Two souls dissolve, in love's abyss.
In the silence, I call out your name,
And in the stillness, your presence, I claim.

For though words may falter, hearts understand,
In the depths of love, where dreams expand.
You're near to my heart, like a gentle beat,
In the symphony of love, where souls meet.

In the absence of rain, the blue rose finds solace true, for in the soil, he discovers a friend so pure and true.

Every word from his broken heart, The soil listen,
A companion in solitude, offering life for tears to glisten.
In this understanding bond, life's essence is revealed, for in the soil's embrace, the blue rose's wounds are healed.

To the soil, my faithful companion,
In your embrace, I find solace, a union.
For what is a picture without some shade,
In darkness and light, our bond is made.

Each moment with you, a precious gift,
In your presence, spirits lift.
The music of nature, an emotion profound,
in every breeze, its melody resound.
It dances on lips, whispers in ears,
In eyes that glisten with joyful tears.
For in the heart, it finds its home,
In the symphony of life, we're not alone.

In the dance of life, the blue rose and soil entwine,
A bond unseen, yet steady through time.
For from the soil's embrace, the rose did spring,
A silent nurturer, like a parent's loving wing.

Through seasons of bloom and moments of grace,
The soil cradles the rose, in its embrace.
And when the time comes, for the rose to rest,
He returns to the soil, fulfilling life's quest.

The soil, a guide, a teacher, a friend,
In life's darkness, it lends a hand to mend.
With strength it provides, in times of despair,
Hope and direction, it offers with care.

In this cycle of birth, growth, and decay,
The bond between rose and soil will forever stay.
For in the end, as the rose turns to dust,
he becomes one with the soil, in nature's trust.

To the birds and trees, the blue rose sings,
Of love's pages, where eternity clings.
You, a book of love, in pages unfurled,
A story to cherish, in a timeless world.

For to gain, one must lose, in life's design,
In the dance of moments, yours and mine.
Yet in my heart, you'll forever reside,
In the depths of love, where souls confide.

Is it always or forever, the word profound,
In the curtains of time, where truths are found.
Forever, with its infinite grace,
Holds the presence of love, in every space.

In love's embrace, there are no ways,
No paths to follow, in its endless maze.
For love is forever and ever more,
In the whispers of time, its essence soar.

In the realm of illusion, the blue rose dreams,
where lost spirits wander, in silent streams.
In this materialistic world of words and thoughts,
Existence is shaped by the soul's deep knots.

Every word, every thought, a creation of our mind,
In this intricate web, our truths we find.
Yet sometimes, words fail to capture the feelings,
Leaving hearts to decipher their own healings.

But amidst this maze, one truth rings clear,
In the depths of love, there's no room for fear.

For I love you, with all that I am,
In my heart, you'll forever stand.

In dreams, the blue rose yearns for the rain's
embrace, a longing deep, in its tranquil space.

You're the breath within, the pulse in my chest,
In your love, my eternal rest.
So stay with me, my love, my light,
For without you, I'm but a soul in night.

In the blue rose's realm, birdsong fills the air,
A symphony of melodies, beyond compare.
Yet as he listens, he longs to join the tune,
But no words emerge, just silence strewn.

His petals may hold a lonely tale,
Yet within his silence, emotions prevail.
For in the language of feeling, he finds his voice,
speaking distinctly without a single noise.

Where spoken words may falter and fail,
Expression of feeling leaves no trail.
His eyes, filled with bliss, gaze upon the sky,
At the birds that sing, clouds that fly.

Words may preach morals, or sow seeds of hate,
Yet at life's end, they hold neither love nor fate.
In the realm of the blue rose, where silence reigns,
True beauty lies, untouched by words' constraints.

To the wind breeze, the blue rose speaks,
Of raindrops falling, in whispered streaks.
From heaven's plane, they come to meet,
With a heartbeat, in love's sweet retreat.

The rain, the heart's song, in gentle words,
Showering love, like singing birds.
As she cascades down, making angels of us,
In her embrace, we find love's trust.

Listening to her rhythm, the soul finds peace,
In the rain's touch, all worries cease.
For as each drop falls, blue rose's heart does stall,
Delighted by rain's words, nature's soul heed their call.

So let the rain shower, let her fall,
In her embrace, I find my all.
For in her gentle touch, I am complete,
In the whispers of rain, my heart does beat.

In the heart of the forest, the blue rose sings,
His melody woven with life's mystical strings.
Each word, each line, a piece of his soul,
A symphony of essence, making the forest whole.
These words, they're more than mere sound;
They carry the whispers of soul profound.
Distributed fragments of self, they flow,
But their true magic, in feeling, does grow.

Bathed in moonlight's gentle glow, the moon and wind draw near, Listening to the blue rose's song in the starry atmosphere.

His melodies may ascend to distant stars above,
A hope that souls will journey to realms of boundless love.

In dreams spun from mere words, life's vast canvas we perceive, Within the blue rose's whispers, worlds of wonder we conceive.

So close your eyes, let the melody surround,
Let the essence of the blue rose be found.
For understanding fades, but feeling remains,
In the forest's soul, where mystery reigns.

In the gentle caress of the wind, a message unfurls, A handwritten letter from the rain, a song of the world.

Each page carries the scent of earth, the whispers of the rain, As the blue rose receives it, his petals unfold, a silent refrain.

The letter speaks of the monsoon's arrival, At the forest's edge, where dreams and hopes revive.

With each word, the rose dances in the breeze, Announcing to the sky, the imminent release.

For in the embrace of rain, lies a promise divine, Each droplet a kiss, a symbol of love's design.

As the blue rose awaits, in anticipation and delight, He knows the rainbow will come, painting the sky bright.

In the hush of the forest, the blue rose stands tall, Listening to the secrets that the raindrops recall.

He knows that with the rain, comes a symphony of sound, Nature's orchestra, in which each note is

found. The scent of the earth, the patter of the rain,
Whispers of life, sung in nature's refrain.

For the blue rose, this is a sacred time,
A moment of connection, in nature's hymn.

As the clouds gather and the sky turns gray,
The blue rose awaits the downpour, come what may.

For in the rain's embrace, he finds solace and peace,
A timeless dance, where worries and woes cease.

In the heart of the foggy mountain's misty embrace, The blue rose finds himself lost in a dreamy space.

With each droplet of rain, a melody is born,
A symphony of nature, where dreams adorn.

In this ethereal realm, where reality fades,
The blue rose dances with the rain in cascading shades.

She paints the sky with hues of blue,
Lost in the moment, in the dream's anew.

But as the night unfolds and the dream begins to wane, The blue rose awakens, his petals soaked with rain.

Yet, in the stillness of the night, he holds onto the dream, For in his essence, lies a truth, a gleam.

For dreams may be fleeting, like stars in the night,
But their impact on the soul burns ever bright.

In the blue rose's heart, the dream lives on,
A reminder of the magic that is never truly gone.

So as he gazes at the sky, watching meteors streak,
The blue rose lays in a dream, so unique.

For in the dreams we weave, lies a world untold,
Where the blue rose dances, in rain and stardust's hold.

In the embrace of the fog, the forest breathes,
A silent symphony, where the soul perceives.
The blue rose, amidst the misty veil,
Sits in quiet reverence, his essence frail.

Yet within his fragile form, a spirit bold,
A beacon of truth, in a world untold.
For in the fog of uncertainty, he finds his way,
Guided by the light of his heart's pure ray.

As the mist wraps around like a comforting shawl,
The blue rose listens to nature's gentle call.
In the whispers of the trees, secrets are shared,
A sacred bond, in the stillness neared.

For in the fog of the moment, truth may be concealed, But in the depths of the soul, it is revealed.

The blue rose, a symbol of resilience and grace,
Navigates through the mist, with steady gaze.
As the fog begins to lift and the day takes flight,
The blue rose remains, a testament to inner light.

In the quiet beside the river's gentle flow,
Blue rose feel its rhythm within, a whispered echo.
Each ripple, each wave, an emotion untold,
As he merge with its essence, his soul unfolds.

The blue rose yearns to see through its eyes, to feel its sway, To be by its side, as it flows each day.

With every beat, blue rose's heart syncs with its tune, in harmony with the river, beneath the moon.

Long to breathe as it does, in perfect sync,
To be one with its flow, no thought to think.

For in its embrace, blue rose find solace true,
Living and dying, as the river's blue.

The blue rose wonders, for we are one, the river and I, Bound by the flow, beneath the sky.

In its currents, I found my home, forever in its embrace, I'll roam.

Beneath the skies that paint tales of the mountain high.

As the river dances, it carries mountain's songs so free, Perhaps a messenger, to send blue rose's fragrance to the rain, the river may agree.

In the stillness of night, with dreams unspoken,
Blue rose searches for love, in darkness unbroken.
Unexplained feelings, in hearts so naive,
Yet through expectations, life finds reprieve.

For in the doorway of expectation, life finds its way,
Guided by dreams, in the light of day.
Whispering hopes, in sleepless nights,
The blue rose finds solace, in life's endless flights.

Amidst the forest's silent sway, the blue rose weeps in disarray, Entwined in love's shattered refrain, Bound by soil, he can't break free from the chain.

Yearning to soar on wings unseen,
To where raindrops dance, so serene,
In dreams he flies, to a realm afar,
Where echoes of rain play on like a distant star.

Amidst the moon's glow, where whispers of stars and rivers flow.

Bound by no limits, no earthly tether,
The blue rose roams, in realms of forever.

But in this realm, where dreams collide,
And hopes and fears forever hide,
The blue rose lingers in silent despair,
As rainless skies whisper tales of love in silent air.

In the depths of introspection, the blue rose ponders, What would I be, if not for this world I wander?

Is it I who fills the blank space with my bloom,
Or does this world, in turn, fill me with its own fume?

Two views collide in the depths of my soul,
Is this world a canvas, with each of us a stroke whole?

Or are we the canvas, waiting to be filled,
By the world's colors, by destiny willed?

Perhaps it's both, a dance of give and take,
Each moment shared, each step we make.
For in this blank space, we find our purpose true,
In the words we speak, in the deeds we do.

So let us embrace this dance of life's grace,
In the blank space, find our rightful place.

For whether we fill it, or it fills us whole,
In this shared journey, we find our soul.

In the moon's soft glow, the blue rose keeps his watch, as shadows dance, mirroring our joys and touch.

With the sun's descent, light begins to wane,
Yet life persists, in the rustle of leaves' refrain.

Life, like a passing cloud, observes the sunset's grand display, as a child sits by, watching worries fade away.

For each day dawns, each moment fleeting fast,
Yet we fail to see the dewdrops glistening,
The moment past.

In the daydream, where shadows play,
The blue rose ponders, in the quiet of the bay.
For life's true essence lies not in fleeting sights,
But in the whispers of nature, on sleepless nights.

So let us embrace the moon's tender light,
And cherish each moment, in the silent night.
For in the dew-kissed grass, life's beauty gleams,
A reminder of existence, in moonlit dreams.

In the stillness of the forest, where shadows play,
The blue rose finds solace in the cool, shaded array.
As sunlight felt in the winds chase,
It illuminates the path, each step a trace.

Rooted to the soil, yet yearning to roam,
The blue rose dreams of a world unknown.
If only he could wander like the wind, so free,
He would explore the depths of his inner sea.

In the rustling leaves and whispering trees,
The blue rose finds his inner peace, a silent ease.
For in the heart of nature's serene domain,
He discovers a refuge from life's mundane.

With each breeze that sweeps through the glade,
The blue rose feels a connection, deep and
unswayed.

In the symphony of nature's song, he finds his
voice, A melody of peace, in which he can rejoice.
His spirit takes flight, exploring the realms of day
and night. In the dance of shadow and light,
He seeks the answers, hidden from sight.

In the quiet of the night, the blue rose dreams,
Of distant galaxies and celestial streams.
With each twinkling star, a hope is spun,
A fabric of dreams, until the night is done.

As the moon ascends, casting its radiant light,
It serves as a beacon in the vast expanse of night.
Dreams take flight, like hues in the starry sky,
Guiding souls through life's journey, up high.

Through the veil of darkness, it finds its way,
Guided by the stars' eternal sway.
In the soul of the night, it finds its home,
Amidst the cosmos, it's free to roam.

The blue rose knows, in his silent sway,
That life's essence lies in the void's array.
For in nothingness, all things find their birth,
In the stillness of the cosmos, all meet their worth.

In the realm where shadows dance with light,
Where day and night blends in endless flight,
There lies a truth, both profound and deep,
In the heart of silence, where secrets sleep.

In the dance of opposites, in the ebb and flow,
The blue rose sees the essence of all that we know.
For light needs darkness, and joy needs pain,
In the colors of existence, they all reign.

But in the quietude of nothingness, all dissolves,
The illusions of life, the puzzles it solves.
For when we find ourselves in that empty space,
We realize that all is one, in its own place.

In the profound depths of life, the blue rose ponders, His origin from nothingness, to the void it wanders.

What will he achieve in this worldly dance,
As moments slip by, leaving little chance?

Worries from the past may cloud his view,
But in nature's embrace, his essence rings true.
Life's meaning found in its purest form,
Amidst the symphony of calm and storm.

Life, an illusion woven with songs and dreams,
Filled with memories that flow in silent streams.
As time draws near to its inevitable end,
What remains are echoes, in the moonlit blend.

In the life's realm, secrets unfold,
In whispers of nature, his stories told.
Through sunlit days and moonlit nights,
His essence sings of life's pure delights.

In the blue rose's outlook, walls rise high,
Man's constructs, where dreams seem to die.
Prisoned within, in hopeless schemes,
He fears the day he becomes a decoration in man's dreams.

Cut from his roots, a mere ornament to display,
In a world of confinement, where dreams decay.
The blue rose shudders at the thought,
Of losing its essence, its beauty wrought.

For in the confines of walls, he sees,
The imprisonment of souls, where freedom flees.
Yearning for open skies, where dreams can soar,
He fears becoming just another adornment, nothing more.

Yet even in captivity, the blue rose dreams of past,
Hope of breaking free at last.
For within its petals lies resilience untamed,
A spirit unbroken, though walls may be framed.

In the gaze of the blue rose, man appears,
Burdened by words, drowning in fears.
Depressed by the weight of worldly speech,
Caught in a cycle, difficult to breach.

Words cascade like a relentless stream,
Drowning out silence, suffocating the dream.
In the blue rose's eyes, He sees the worldly role,
Of words spoken in haste, taking their toll.

For in the quiet of nature, where peace resides,
Man finds solace, where noise subsides.

Yet in the unpleasant sounds, he's lost, In a sea of chatter, his spirit become shattered.

The blue rose longs for moments of still,
Where words are few, but meaning fill.
For in the silence, true understanding lies,
Where hearts connect, beneath the skies.

In the blue rose's view, man is weighed down,
By the burden of money, his heart's crown.
Caught in a web of greediness,
He forsakes simplicity, forsakes the joyfulness.

Driven by the desire for wealth and acclaim,
He loses touch with what truly inflames.
His soul, once free, now shackled tight,
To the pursuit of riches, blinding his sight.

In the midst of opulence, the blue rose sighs,
Watching as man's true essence slowly dies.
For in the facade of world's flair,
He loses touch with what's truly rare.

Amidst the glitter and the shine,
The blue rose longs for a simpler time.

Where value lies not in possessions amassed,
But in moments shared, destined to last, a bliss that life asks.

For in the shadow of wealth's heavy load,
Man forgets the beauty of the untold.

And the blue rose weeps for what's been lost,
In the pursuit of riches, nature have paid a cost.

In the canvas of existence, the blue rose spies,
The intricate fabric of human highs and sighs.
With emotions vast, their souls unfold,
In every hue and shade, a story untold.

Their intentions, like colors, vary and blend,
Some in vibrant hues, others at life's end.
Yet amidst the chaos, a journey prevails,
A quest for meaning, as the soul unveils.

Each stroke of life's brush, a vivid display,
Some vibrant and bold, others in shades of gray.
But in every stroke, there lies a tale,
Of triumph and loss, where hearts prevail.

For even in brokenness, there's a glimmer of light,
A spark of hope, in the darkest of night.
They dream of tomorrows, yet to come,
As they dance with shadows, under the sun.

Though time may weather, and trials may sway,
Their spirits endure, in the grand ballet.

In the end, they surrender, to life's grand design,
With grace and dignity, they bid goodbye.

So the blue rose observes, with reverence and grace,
The wonders of humanity, in every trace.

For in their journey, they find their way,
Through colors and hues, in life's grand ballet.

In the dance of life, the blue rose spies,
Smiling faces that hide the tears in their eyes.
In the fleeting moments of joy, they find release,
A respite from worries, a moment of peace.

But behind the mask, their struggles lie,
In the depths of their hearts, where emotions fly.
They endure the trials, the burdens they bear,
Yet in their smiles, a glimmer of care.

For the mountains may move, and the trees may sway, But their smiles remain, come what may.

It's a facade they wear, for the world to see,
A shield against pain, a cloak of glee.

Yet the blue rose sees beyond the guise,
To the souls beneath, where truth lies.
Amidst their laughter and their transient elegance,
They discover comfort in life's swift exuberance.

So let them smile, let them be free,
For in their laughter, lies their glee.
The blue rose watches, with tender gaze,
As humanity dances, in life's maze.

In the living room's confines, a blue rose stands,
Enclosed by walls, like endless hands.
In a few fleeting days, he may depart,
leaving behind his beauty, a memory at heart.

But in his aging grace, he dreams of flight,
Where petals may fall, yet take to the height.
For within his soul, a winged companion lies,
Whispering of dreams that reach the skies.

Though his form may fade, his spirit gleams,
Filled with an everlasting dream.
To soar beyond walls, where freedom reigns,
A testament to life, amidst earthly chains.

Even as his petals scatter, carried by the breeze,
The blue rose's spirit soars, beyond earthly shores.

With the fear of death lurking, that the sun may not shine, and the blue rose may miss the rain, a sorrowful sign.
He longs to listen to the birds' songs and the stream's gentle flow, Yet filled with the essence of an everlasting dream, he finds solace, even so.

The blue rose, anxious, witnessing mankind's desperate plight, Imprisoned in their own fears, in the darkness of night.

Bound by despair, depression, and anxiety's thrall, He sees the web of humanity's desperation sprawl.

In the room of walls, where ambitions lead astray, Humans chase dreams, losing life's essence in their fray.

As the blue rose stands witness to this futile chase, He mourns the loss of beauty, in life's relentless race.

Where fallen petals reclaim the sky. But amidst the constructs of love and hate's bind, Humans build walls of words, trapping the mind.

For within the cage of emotions they weave, Freedom remains elusive, a distant reprieve.

In the quiet of the room, the pen takes flight,
A faithful companion in the still of the night.
With every stroke, emotions flow free,
Captured on pages, for all to see.

Each paragraph, a journey's start,
Each dot a pause, a beat of the heart.
Each comma a breath, a moment's pause,
In the symphony of thoughts, without a cause.

In the dance of ink upon the page,
The pen becomes the poet's sage.
With each stroke, a story unfurls,
Capturing the essence of the world's whirls.

But in the end, words fall short, of the depths of silence. In the absence of sound, in the absence of light, The blue rose blooms, in silent might.

For in the quiet, the blue rose knows,
The true essence of life, in silence it shows.

Amidst the pages of time, the blue rose peers,
Where memories shimmer like stars, free from fears.

He ponders the words, now lost to the past,
Do they hold meaning, or are they fading fast?

In a world unaware of its own heart's beat,
Man shows love by the roses he fleet.

With each rose cut, a love professed,
A death in bloom, a heart confessed.

Yet within the book's silent face,
Do these words echo, leaving a trace?

Each page a story, each word a sigh,
Capturing moments that once flew by.

Though the world may forget, the book remembers true, In its timeless arm’s, old memories anew.

In the act of love, a rose is cut,
A gift bestowed, without rebut.
But within the book's silent keep,
Do these gestures find their place to sleep?

For love expressed in petals' bloom,
Captured in pages, in silent room.
Yet the book holds secrets, untold and deep,
In its quiet refuge, emotions seep.

Book like a petals, adorns each page,
A silent sonnet, and unspoken sage,
Yet beneath the words, what remains unsaid?
In the book's, ink is its heart where love is spread.

Words unspoken, dreams untold,
In the book soul's reflections, unfold.
A silent witness to love's fleeting spark,
Preserved in pages, even when worlds grow dark.

As the blue rose delves deeper into the realms of dreams, he find himself lost in their ethereal streams.

Are they mere illusions or glimpses of truth?
In the arms of dream, i find eternal youth.

Each dream, a world of its own creation,
A fabric woven with imagination.
They whisper secrets of the heart,
Guiding me on this mysterious art.

In dreams, I am both creator and muse,
Crafting stories with nothing to lose.
They paint the canvas of my soul,
A symphony of colors, making me whole.

So I'll embrace my dreams, both wild and free,
For within them, I find the truest me.
They may be elusive, yet they are real,
A reflection of all I dare to feel.

In the shadows, the blue rose observes,
A man dons masks, his true self preserved.
In a world where dreams seem lost, unreal,
His feelings, genuine, beneath the mask's seal.

Like a book devoid of words, silent yet real,
In this world, dreams lay dormant, concealed.
Pages blank, awaiting tales untold,
As the world's stage unfolds, stories unfold.

Bound by rules, freedom but a dream,
A caged bird, longing to break free, it seems.
Yet within the blue rose's silent gaze,
Hope flickers, in the darkest of days.

In the depths of silence, where truth resides,
The blue rose finds solace, where dreams coincide.
For in the quiet, away from the world's glare,
He discovers freedom, beyond compare.

In the realm of dreams, where hearts are free,
The blue rose dances, in wild ecstasy.
No masks, no rules, just pure, boundless flight,
In the canvas of dreams, he finds his light.

The blue rose listens to a voice from the past,
A memory, a sound, a song that lasts.
Though fleeting, its presence lingers on,
In the fragrance of the present, a feeling strong.

In the dance of time, where moments sway,
The blue rose finds himself in the grand display.
For in each melody, each note that rings,
Lies a tale of life, of ordinary things.

And so he listens, with petals unfurled,
To the symphony of life, in this vast world.

In the whispers of the wind, the songs of the stream, The blue rose finds his place, in this eternal dream.

As the echoes of the past fade away,
The future beckons, a strain to stay.
Yet in the fragrance of the present's hold,
The blue rose finds solace, in stories untold.

In life's canvas, contrasts doth play,
Opposites dance in the light of day.
The blue rose sees his thorns, stark and bold,
A counterpart to his petals, soft and untold.

Love and pain, intertwined they be,
In the curtains of life, for all to see.
For where there is joy, there lies sorrow,
In every dawn, there's a twilight to borrow.

It's in the balance of opposites we find,
The very essence of our humankind.
For in the contrast, life's meaning is revealed,
In the interplay of light and shadow, our fate is sealed.

As love finds its meaning in the depths of despair,
A symphony of contrasts, woven with care.
For in the thorns, the darkness doth reside,
Yet without their presence, light would not abide.

The darkness and the light, For in their union, our souls take flight. In the balance of opposites, we discover, The true beauty of life.

In the quiet realm where the blue rose roams,
He ponders the depth of human tones.

For tears and laughter, words and sighs,
Can never truly express what lies.
In melodies sung and canvases drawn,
Our souls find solace, our spirits dawn.

For in the realm of art and song,
Our deepest truths forever belong.
Though they too have their bounds and bars,
They unlock the gates to our inner stars.

In colors painted and notes that ring,
We find the truth of everything.

So let us cherish this boundless art,
And let it heal each wounded heart.
For in the depths of human tones,
We find the beauty of our own.

In the curtains of life, the blue rose discerns,
The hues and shades of human yearns.
With strokes of emotions, they paint their way,
Each color a tale, in the grand display.

Some shine bright with hopes untold,
While others wander in shadows, cold.
Their hearts may break, their spirits bend,
Yet still, they dream, until the end.

For in the journey of souls, there lies a grace,
A beauty in the struggle, a sacred space.
Each life, is unique, in its own right,
Fading gracefully into the eternal night.

So the blue rose watches, with silent awe,
As human beings write their story, raw.
In every brushstroke, in every sigh,
Lies the essence of life, before goodbye.

At the autumn's gate, the blue rose watches leaves descend, Witnessing the quiet act of nature, where silence finds its blend.

To others, silence may seem a mere absence of sound, But to the blue rose, it's a song profound.

For in the rustling leaves and the whispering breeze, Silence speaks it own tune, with effortless ease.

It reaches beyond words, beyond what's explained, In the uncharted realms, where mysteries are contained.

True silence lies not in the absence of noise,
But in the depths of nature's tranquil poise.

And as leaves fall gently, in the autumn's soft breeze, The blue rose finds solace, in silence that frees.

Nature's song finds souls alone, For in the quietude of self, true peace is known.

Silence speaks in the soul's quiet hum, A symphony of solitude, where hearts find freedom to become.

With each day that passes, the blue rose sees,
A new morning dawn, painting skies with ease.
As night falls, the moon and stars appear,
Whispering secrets, calming every fear.

World has mere words we often convey,
Yet in silence, they find their way.
Time speaks for us in the acts we play,

The actions remain unclear,
But in the stillness, whispers of hope draw near.
Uncertain of direction, we wander and sway,
Wondering what the future will lay.

Yet in the silence, our words fade away,
Lost in the quiet, where truths hold sway.
For in the silence that surrounds, words may fail,
But in the heart's quiet, truths prevail.

And as the blue rose ponders what the future may hold, He finds solace in the silence, where mysteries unfold.

Watching a rustling flower, the blue rose ponders,
What life has in its wonders.
In the curtains of time, where moments weave,
One certainty remains, in death, we all must leave.

Death, the silent culmination of life's fleeting dance, Holding within it every chance, Every combination, every endeavor,
Yet we struggle to accept it, now and forever.

But within the passage of time, a chance for rebirth,
A chance for life to redefine its worth.

For though death may seem final, its silence profound, In the moments we cherish, new possibilities abound.

The life's uncertainty, its ebb and flow,
For in each fleeting moment, new seeds of hope may sow.

And as the blue rose contemplates time's mysteries deep, He finds solace in the silence, where new possibilities sleep.

In the yearning of the blue rose to meet the rain,
He falls down, unseen, yet cries in vain.
Tears cascade, but the world remains blind,
Only the thunder of sorrow, echoes in mind.

As rain falls, eyes still, unheard tears flow,
In the silence, the world fails to know.
Hiding tears in the rain, a silent plea,
For a whisper of love, to set the heart free.

But still, the world fails to understand,
The depths of emotion, the touch of love's hand.
In the quiet downpour, the blue rose waits,
Hoping for the world to feel, before it's too late.
As the rain returns, bringing peace anew,
The blue rose finds solace, his final view.

Yet, the world remains oblivious to the tears that cry. a silent tear, a whisper of love, lost in soil, holds dear he sigh.

In the moonlit sky wishes come true in dreams bright, As the dying rose sings its last song in the night.

Dear Reader,

Within the delicate pages of "Melodies of life of a Blue Rose," I invite you to wander through the garden of verse, where every line is a petal unfurling, revealing the beauty and complexity of both nature's splendor and the human heart's tender bloom.

Poetry, like nature itself, speaks in whispers and sighs, in the subtle language of wind and water, of shadow and light. It is a mirror held up to the soul, reflecting our deepest joys and sorrows, our most profound longings and fleeting moments of grace.

As you immerse yourself in the verses woven within these pages, may you find solace in the rhythm of each stanza, in the melody of each word. Let each poem be a sanctuary where you can pause, breathe, and listen to the whispers of the wind, to the song of the stars, to the echoes of your own heart.

Should you feel moved to linger a little longer on a particular poem, or if a verse sparks a question or a reflection, I encourage you to reach out. Poetry is a dialogue, a dance between poet and reader, and your thoughts and musings are cherished companions on this lyrical journey.

And should inspiration strike, if you find yourself weaving your own verses in response to the ones you encounter here, know that your voice is a vital thread in the rich fabric of poetic expression.

With gratitude for your presence on this poetic odyssey,

Dipankur Bodwal

dipankurbodwal@gmail.com

www.ingramcontent.com/pod-product-compliance
Lightning Source LLC
LaVergne TN
LVHW021258160826
845679LV00001B/119

* 9 7 8 9 3 3 4 0 3 2 1 8 5 *